ADVENTURE 1

HOME IS NOT A CARDBOARD BOX

ELLY MOSSMAN

ISBN: 978-1-990414-47-3

E-book: 978-1-990414-46-6

INDEX

For all the kitties that have found good homes,
and all the people who made it happen.

Adopting a pet is a commitment, no matter how you look at it. Take it from me, it's like having another kid in the house... they become part of the family, with all the perks and problems that come with it!

 A lot of people say, *"It's just a cat!"* when I'm crying over another one. Yup. Other people's cats may be *"just cats"*, but not ours.

Ours are family, warts and all. Bebe can be a handful. She has issues, lots of them. But she's the most loving kitty we've ever had. She loves everybody, strangers and friends, greeting them at the door, and saying goodbye when they leave. She loves to travel and is at home anywhere, be it car, boat or motel room. She's not afraid of anything, not even the vacuum cleaner! Whoever dumped her missed out on the sweetest cat there ever was. It's their loss.

She knows she's spoiled. She has us well trained.

I wouldn't have it any other way!

EDIT: 2024

Since this was written, Bebe has succumbed to her respiratory issues, and, at the age of 14 has crossed that rainbow bridge. We miss her terribly, but she will live on in these books. You'll enjoy her adventures, just like we did.

ADVENTURE 1
HOME IS NOT A
CARDBOARD BOX

1 - THE BOX IN THE WOODS

Sister kitten looked at brother with a worried look in her eye. Brother looked back at his sister with an equally troubled expression. Both of them sat in a cardboard box that stood at the edge of a lonely, mountain road. They had no idea why they were there, or what to do next. Both of them were born in the middle of the summer. Nobody knows where.

Their adventures began when they were very little.

It looked like somebody left them by the side of the road. Nobody knows who. This was a very mean thing to do, but they did it anyway. And, nobody knows why.

They were alone and scared in the cardboard box, and glad that they had each other.   It was now fall, and things were beginning to cool down. For a while they played in the grass beside the road until they got tired. It was getting dark earlier than ever.

"I'm hungry!" said Sister kitten. "I haven't had any dinner."

"Me too!" said Brother kitten. "I wish Mommy was here! I wonder if I can find food to eat?"

While Sister waited, Brother tried to hunt, but he came back with nothing because he didn't know how to hunt. They drank some water from a muddy puddle, curled up together in the box and went to sleep, tired cold and hungry. Sister didn't feel well.

By the next morning they were even hungrier, and this time Sister said to Brother, "It's my turn to find something to eat." She jumped out of the cardboard box and ran a little way down the road, looking under the rocks as she went. But, she found nothing to eat under there.

She peeked under a bush, but nobody left a sandwich, or even a tiny scrap of macaroni and cheese for them. She parted the tall grass and hoped maybe she would find half a cookie or, if she was lucky, a whole sardine!

She was still crouched down in the grass when she heard a horrible screech high above her head. The next thing she knew, a dark bundle of whirring feathers took the sun away. Something deep inside of herself told her to MOVE NOW! She made a lightning-fast dive to the underside of a thick pine branch, and felt something skim the end of her tail and she dove. But, she was safe.

What was that?

"Wow! That was CLOSE!" a voice called out from under a nearby bush. Sister stared at the bush. Could bushes talk? A pair of bright black eyes stared back at her. The eyes became part of a funny-looking

face that also had pointy little ears, a pointy nose … and it was wearing a mask!

"Who are you?" she asked the funny looking creature, "And what was that thing coming out of the sky?"

"That.." said Raccoon, "..was an eagle! And you were almost dinner. Don't you know better than to stay out in the open in the woods?" Then he advised Sister, "Always stay under cover, otherwise Eagle can come swooping down to pick you up, and turn you into a delicious meal!"

"I didn't know that. I'm not even supposed to be here!" cried poor Sister. "Somebody just left us out in the woods, and now I'm trying to find something to eat."

"Well, just be careful." advised Raccoon, and off he waddled into the bushes.

"Wait, wait!" cried Sister after him. "Can't you help me find some food?" But Raccoon was long gone.

2 - THE LONG, SLITHERY THING

Poor Sister sighed, wishing that Raccoon had been a little more patient, but she followed his advice and stayed under the bushes and trees. The only thing she found was an old orange peel, and that didn't taste very good.

Just as she was deciding whether Brother might like the orange peel, she saw a long, slithery thing slide in front of her. "Hello," it said. Was it something to eat?

Well! Sister couldn't begin to think about eating something that said "hello" to her ... so, she said "hello" back.

"What are you doing out in the middle of these woods?" asked the long, slithery thing.

"Somebody left me and Brother in a cardboard box," answered Sister, "and I don't think it was a very nice thing to do. Now we're very hungry and we can't find anything to eat!"

Then Sister asked the long thing, "What are you? You have no feet."

"*Tch, tch, tch,*" said the long, slithery thing, "where are your manners? I'm a snake. Haven't you ever seen a snake before?"

"No," said Sister, "I haven't."

"I slide along the ground using my tummy muscles. Very clever, don't you think?" Sister had to agree. Oh yes, very clever indeed.

"Can I do that?" she asked. Without waiting for an answer, Sister dropped down on her tummy and wriggled through the dirt. It wasn't easy, and she looked just a little silly. Snake started to laugh.

"Oh, you are bonkers, with your feet sticking out from all sides! Look at your tummy. Now you're all dirty!" And Snake laughed and laughed.

Sister sat up, suddenly tired, hungry and not feeling very well at all. She started to cry. Snake was sorry that he'd laughed at her, and sad that she was hungry. He thought and thought. Suddenly, he knew what to do!

"Take me back to Brother in the box." ordered Snake. Sister got up and ran all the way back to Brother, Snake slithering and sliding along behind. Brother was sound asleep and Sister woke him up.

"Did you find something to eat?" asked Brother sleepily, "I'm hungrier than ever!"

"I found a friend," answered Sister. "This is Snake."

"Hello Snake. Can you help us find something to eat?" asked Brother hopefully of Snake.

"No, but, I have a better idea. Stay here in the box and wait until I come back." he answered the poor hungry kittens.

Snake slid away and disappeared from sight. Sister and Brother looked at each other. "I wonder if he'll bring back something to eat?" wondered Sister.

"Oh, you are bonkers!" laughed Brother, "didn't he say say he had a better idea?"

"What could be better than eating?" grumbled Sister.

It started to rain while Sister and Brother sat in the box, waiting for Snake. They crouched down, but the box had no top, so the rain made them wet anyway. It didn't make a very good house.

"I hope Snake comes back soon with his good idea!" wailed Sister. "I don't like getting wet, I'm already dirty, and I don't feel good!"

"Ah-ah-AAA-CHOOOO!!" She let out a huge sneeze. Her eyes started getting watery, and her nose was all stuffed up. This was no good at all!

Finally the rain stopped. Sister and Brother sat shivering in the box, hungrier, colder and more tired than they'd ever been, waiting for Snake to come back.

Meanwhile, Snake had slipped and slithered down the mountain road. He worried a bit when it started to rain, but he kept looking and looking for …. and yes, finally he saw what he wanted. A man and a dog came walking up the road, the man whistling. The dog was snuffling at everything and everywhere as she went.

Snake got as close as he dared to Dog, and shouted at the top of his lungs, **"WOO-HOO!"** as loud and as long as he could.

Dog picked up her ears.

"What is it girl, what do you hear?" asked the man.

"Woof!" said Dog, and began running hard.

Luckily Snake was faster than Dog as he slithered and slid his way back to the cardboard box. Dog chased hard behind Snake, and the man chased hard after Dog. With the box now in sight, the last stretch up the mountain road seemed the longest of all, as Snake, panting, slithered almost up to it.

At the last second, he slid away into the tall grass beside the road. Dog, now curious about the box, screeched to a halt and began sniffing around it. She smelled cat, which was almost as good as squirrel!

3 - THE RESCUE MONSTER

A dark shadow fell over Sister and Brother as they sat in the box. After the rain had stopped the sun peeked out just a little, to warm them up a bit. So, the two of them had climbed out of the box to dry off. Then they'd chased a ray of sunshine. When they got tired, they'd climbed back into the box for a snooze.

Now suddenly, the sun disappeared again, and they crouched, shivering in shadow … and something else!

"Woof!" said Dog. Sister started crying again, and tried to hide behind brother, who was just as scared. What toothy monster was this?

The man finally caught up with Dog and peered over her shoulder at two dirty, partly wet kittens. "What have you got here, girl? What did you find?"

"Kittens!" said Dog. But all the man understood was, "Wuf!" The man picked up the shivering Sister and Brother, and put them under his jacket. "There," he said, "that might be a bit warmer for you."

Under the coat Sister and Brother whispered to each other. "I don't know whether this is good or bad." whispered Brother.

"I just hope we get something to eat. Maybe I'll feel better." answered Sister. "I wonder where we're going … and what is that big fuzzy thing that said *wuf*?"

"It couldn't be anything like Snake," replied Brother, "it has four legs like us!" Sister peeked out from under the jacket. "Hello! What are you? Are you anything like Snake?" she asked Dog, who was walking alongside.

"What? Oh, you are bonkers!" laughed Dog. "I'm a dog! Haven't you ever seen a dog before?"

Before Sister could answer, the man stopped in front of a big pickup truck, almost like the one that had carried them up the mountain road. He opened his coat and dropped both of them into an old box sitting on the seat of the truck. It was just like the box they'd sat in, riding up to the mountain road! Sister remembered how they were dumped at the end of the ride.

"Oh NO! This is bad! This is really, really bad!" cried Sister. Then she sneezed really loud again… "Ah-Ah-A-*Achooo!*" The man patted her head gently. "It's OK little kitten, I'm bringing you to the Shelter." Brother thought that sounded like a good thing, so he tried to comfort Sister as they bounced away in the truck, with Dog watching over them.

After what seemed like the longest time, they felt the truck stop. The box was lifted out of the truck, and they were carried into a building. It smelled funny. The two frightened kittens heard voices, and crouched down in the box. Then they heard the man's voice say, "I was out walking the dog on the mountain, and found these two beside the road."

There were more voices and lots of other strange sounds. Suddenly they were lifted out of the box with gentle hands, and found themselves in a huge room with lots and lots of other cats. Big ones, little ones, orange ones, black ones, striped and splotchy, all colours and kinds. There were all kinds of smells too, but one smell had Sister's attention. Food!

Sister was put down on the floor in front of a bowl of wonderful-smelling food. She was so hungry there was no stopping her, as she ate and ate. Oh, it tasted like the best thing ever! A bowl of nice, fresh water was next. No more muddy puddles to drink out of. Fresh water tasted wonderful too. Brother was put down at the bowl of food, and he too ate and ate.

Afterwards the two kittens washed themselves clean and dry, just like Mommy had taught them, and then they curled up on a beanbag together and fell fast sleep. "I forgot to thank Snake ..." Sister mumbled as she fell asleep, but Brother was already snoring.

4 - FRIENDS IN THE SHELTER

Sister woke up the next morning and wondered where she was. Everything looked and smelled strange. Other cats were walking around, or stretching from a long night's sleep. Brother was nowhere in sight. He was probably somewhere solving mysteries and looking for adventure. The food dish was still where it was yesterday, and there was still food in it! Sister jumped off the beanbag and ran to eat before it disappeared.

"You don't have to gobble!" said a husky voice in her ear. "There will always be food when you need it." Sister jumped, startled. Beside her stood a very large fluffy cat with more colours than she'd ever seen in her life!

"You're new here, aren't you? My name's Fuzzy. What's yours?"

"I-I don't know what my name is, nobody gave me one." Sister replied.

"Oh yes, you would have been given a name when you got here. If you listen when they talk to you, you will learn what your name is."

Sister promised she would, and then began asking questions. "What is this place? Is my Mommy here too? I miss Mommy. Where's Brother …?"

Fuzzy started to laugh, "Oh my, so many questions! One at a time please!"

"Another silly cat to feed!" growled a second voice from behind her. This interruption was so gruff that Sister jumped again. The grumpy voice belonged to a big, gray tomcat. He looked mean.

"Just stay out of my way, and don't come near the food bowl when I'm eating."

Fuzzy planted herself between Sister and the big gray cat. "Grumblebutt, you're always snarling at the newcomers. Leave her alone! She's just a baby!"

"I am not a baby!" announced Sister, pulling herself up to her full height. "I'm already a big girl! See how tall I a… a-ah ahhhh-CHOOO!"

"You are bonkers!" answered Grumblebutt, "That's what I'm calling you, Bonkers! Booong-kerrrsss!" But before sister could answer back, a person walked into the room and picked her up.

"There you are Belle! Is this big boy bothering you?" asked the Shelter Lady.

Sister answered, "Yes he is! And he's very rude too!" Then Sister realized she'd been called a name! Bell? Her name was Bell, like the bell she remembered from the front door of the house where she lived with Mommy. She said it over and over in her head, but somehow, it didn't sound right.

"I don't feel like a bell," she said to the Shelter Lady, but of course, all the Shelter Lady understood was "Me-ew, chrrup, chrrp, mew!"

"Come with me," said Shelter Lady, "the doctor wants to see you." And off they went.

Doctor looked Belle over very carefully. He poked and prodded, and took Belle's temperature, which she didn't like at all. He looked under her eyelids, and gave her some medicine in a needle. Belle grumbled and squirmed a little. She even cried a little when she felt the needle, but really, it didn't hurt, she was just a little scared, and she was, after all, only a baby.

"This little girl has a cold, and an infection," She heard Doctor tell Shelter Lady. Doctor, meanwhile, scratched Belle behind the ears and under her chin, which felt good, almost as good as Mommy's kisses. When Doctor stopped, she said, "Do that some more. I like that!"

But, of course, all Doctor understood was "Me-ew, chrrup, chrrp, mew!"

Belle wanted to talk to Fuzzy again and ask her about Brother. She wanted to find out what name he'd been given. But, instead of going back to the big room with all the cats, Shelter Lady took her to a small room with lots of little spaces, each with a bed, bowls of food and water, and a litter box.

"You'll stay here for a while, until you feel better," Shelter Lady told her. Belle got another scratch behind the ears, and then she left, closing the door behind her.

A voice squeaked from somewhere in the far corner of the Room-With-Lots-Of-Little-Spaces, "Are you sick too?" Belle couldn't see where the tiny voice was coming from. She peered into the darker corners.

"I-I guess so." Belle answered carefully, looking around as she talked, "I really don't feel that good … where are you? I don't see you!"

"I'm sick too," said the tiny voice, "but I'm getting better, and so will you."

The medicine was making Belle sleepy, and her eyelids were beginning to droop. There was a ritching sound in one corner of the little space right across from her's, and a wee gray kitten poked her head up from behind a gray-blue blanket. "You probably don't see me because I'm still so little."

Belle made a huge yawn as she asked, "What's your name? Mine's Bell, but I really don't feel like a bell."

And before Tid-Bit could answer - because that was her name - Belle was fast asleep.

5 - PLEASE ADOPT ME!

Belle woke up with a start, and once again, wasn't sure where she was. She'd been dreaming about a tiny voice, a long slithery snake that said 'Woof!', and a huge cardboard box that turned into a big, purple cat that wouldn't let her eat! It was all very confusing. She thought she could still hear the tiny voice saying, "I'm so glad you're awake! Now I have someone to talk to!"

Who did that voice belong to? She blinked a few times, sat up and looked around again. Did she dream the voice, or was it real?

"Are you awake?" asked the voice again.

"Uh .. Y-yes .. I think so. Are you real, or am I dreaming?" Belle asked the shadows.

"Of course I'm real! Look!" It was then that she noticed a little gray head peeking from behind a blanket, in the space across the narrow hall.

"Oh! Who are you?" she said, more out of shock than anything else at seeing such a tiny creature in a place like this.

"They call me Tid-Bit because I'm so little. And I'm still so little because I've been very sick," said the wee thing, "but, I'm getting better!"

Just then the door opened and a man came in, saying, "So, who do we have here?" He looked at a sheet of paper. "Ah! We have Belle and Tid-Bit. Are you two getting along?" He didn't wait for an answer. "Good! Let's look at the new-comer first then, shall we?" And without further ado, the new-comer, Belle was carried out to another funny-smelling room, for another poke, prod and temperature-taking.

It was the second of many visits that she got while in the shelter, sometimes by the Doctor, and sometimes by one of the other people who worked there.

She discovered that everybody scratched her behind the ears and under her chin. She loved it, and waited eagerly for each scratch.

Belle stayed in the room with lots of little spaces all the while she was sick. Finally, when she was better she was brought back into the big room with all the cats. There she found Brother playing with a ball. Oh my, how big he'd grown!

"There you are!" she exclaimed. "I've been sick, so I was in a room all my own. I met Tid-Bit. What have you been doing? Did they give you a name?"

Brother started laughing, "I'll bet they named you 'Chatty'. You must be feeling better, you're talking so much."

Then Brother answered her questions. "Hope you're all better now. Wow, you're lucky to have a room all your own! I have to share mine with a whole lot of other cats. I've been doing a lot of exploring and playing, and eating! I'm called 'Buster' now. I think it suits me!"

Belle sighed, "My name is Bell, but I still don't feel like a bell.

"That's a problem," said Buster, "I don't know how to fix that one."

They played together and slept on the beanbag, snuggling together as kittens will do. But, when Belle started to sneeze again, she had to spend more time in the room with lots of little spaces.

She never really got better. Sometimes it was worse. Her eyes would get all gooey and crusted over. She would sneeze and sneeze until her nose was all sore and red. On the days when she was sick, she would either spend her time in the room with lots of little spaces. Or, sometimes, when she was really sick, she'd go home with Mandy the Shelter Lady.

On those days, Mandy would tell her special guest all about how the animals in the shelter were homeless, and that one day all these homeless animals would be adopted one by one by someone nice, who loved animals and wanted one to live with them in their very own forever home. That sounded wonderful to Belle; someone to love her and share their cozy home! Maybe they would also give her a name that fit.

On good days she'd play and sleep in the big room with all the cats. She would always sleep on the beanbag with Buster, and that became their spot.

But the day came when Buster was adopted. Belle was glad he was going to live with people who would be kind to him.

Every day after that, she would watch as people came in to look at all the cats in the big room with all the cats. They'd all be picked up and stroked, and then one of them would be taken out to the room at

the front door. Finally, the lucky kitty would ride away in a car or truck. Even Tid-Bit, who got better and much bigger, was adopted by a tiny little girl and her Daddy.

But it never happened to Belle.

She would sometimes dream of living forever with Mandy. But, after a few days at Mandy's house and getting better, she was always taken back to the shelter. One day she caught sight of herself in a mirror, and thought, "No wonder nobody adopts me. With my runny nose and crusted over eye, I look like a lot of trouble! Who would want to adopt me?"

Poor Belle felt so lonely. Fuzzy would sit and talk with her, trying to cheer her up, and make sure Grumblebutt wasn't being a bully. Sometimes Belle would play with some of the other cats, or go out to the veranda room, where it almost felt like "outside", but not really.

Finally, even Fuzzy was adopted, and Belle was lonelier than ever. She sat on her beanbag and made sure she stayed out of Grumblebutt's way. Day after day she would watch as people came and went back to their homes somewhere, carrying kitties in their carriers.

Fall turned to winter, and winter was on its way to becoming spring. She finally believed that the shelter would be her forever home. She actually began to enjoy all the company of the cats that came and went. Each one had their own story.

There was Bruiser, a fluffy gray, whose family had moved away, and couldn't take him with them.

A tabby, Skittles had an owner who never fed or cared for her properly, so the shelter had rescued her.

Beautiful Missy had been abandoned, and was found scrounging for food in a garbage can. She had been brought to the shelter by a nice lady who just couldn't keep her.

There was even Bradley, the marmalade cat, who'd been hurt so badly by someone playing rough, that his leg had been broken!

They were all adopted out again one by one, and Belle was happy that they'd found good homes.

But nobody came to adopt her.

6 - MAKE YOURSELF AT HOME!

By now, Belle, who still didn't feel like a bell, had grown a lot. She'd become a big, full-grown cat. She began to expect that the shelter was her forever home, and was sound asleep on the beanbag. One moment she was dreaming about Snake and a wet cardboard box, and the next, somebody was tickling her tummy! Thinking it was one of the shelter people, she hung on to the hand, wanting more scratches, and she heard a voice say, "Oh, this one is gentle!"

It was a new voice, one she had never heard before, and she opened her eyes to look. As she did, she felt herself being picked up and

snuggled. There were two people looking at her, and her heart began to beat faster!

A man and a lady were paying attention to her! Her eye was still a bit crusty-looking, and she was snuffling a little, but they were looking at her! She listened as Mandy talked to the man and the lady about her. She heard Mandy telling them that Belle would always have problems with weepy eyes and a runny nose. Oh no!

Finally, the lady put her back into the bean bag and they walked away. She curled back up into a little ball, and decided to ignore them. She just knew they didn't want her anyway, so she decided she didn't care.

She watched out of the corner of her eye, as the couple walked to the room beside the front door and talk to Mandy. They talked to her for a long time, but Belle couldn't hear what they were saying. She closed her eyes. It didn't matter. Nobody wanted her. This was her home now. She just didn't care. And without a concern, she went to sleep.

Later that day Belle heard the same voices. The man and the lady came back, and they had a blue travel carrier with them. They must have decided on which kitty they wanted. She wondered who the lucky one was this time. It wouldn't be her. It would be some other lucky cat, but she didn't care. Nope. She didn't care at all!

Then, Mandy, the man and the lady crossed the big room with all the cats ... and stopped right there in front of her. Mandy picked her up!

"You're going to your forever home, Belle!" she said.

WHAT?! Belle could hardly believe it!

"These are really nice people. You're a very lucky kitty!"

REALLY?? She still couldn't believe it!

"Now, promise me you're going to behave yourself." Mandy sternly asked her.

Belle couldn't believe her ears. She was being adopted! Of *course* she was going to behave herself. She wasn't that bonkers!

"Are you joking? Of course I will!" she cried. But all Mandy understood was, "Me-ow, Chrrup-Chrrp, Meow!".

After all the paperwork was done, her new Mum put her into the blue travel carrier, her new Pa, who Mum called 'Captain', got behind the wheel of the car, and off they went. She wondered if there would be food to eat. She wondered if there would be other kitties there. She wondered if she was really going to a forever home.

When they arrived at her new home, the blue travel carrier was brought indoors and unzipped.

"Out you go sweetie, this is your new home now. Feel free to explore." said Mum. Belle looked around and thought to herself, "I wonder if I'll really stay here forever? It sounded like forever, but I'm not sure. Why would they pick me?"

Mum then put her in front of two dishes, one with food and one with water. "This is where your food is kept." she said. She sniffed the dish. It smelled good, so she had a nibble. "Very good!" said Mum.

Next, Mum picked her up and took her into another small room. "Here is your litter box!" she said, as she dropped her into a box filled with sand. She dug her paw through it and sniffed. It smelled like just the place for her, and hopped out. She knew what to do there! "Very good!" remarked Mum.

I'll let you explore a little more, Belle. This is your home now, too." said Mum then.

"Can I live here forever?" she asked her new Mum, but of course, all Mum understood was, "Me-ow, chrrup-chrrp, meow!"

Mum laughed at all the chattering, though. "My, you're just a chatty thing, aren't you? That's just wonderful! I love chatty kitties."

As she eyed the open bedroom door, thinking she should go explore that new room, the man called 'Captain' spoke up, "The name 'Belle' just doesn't fit her, don't you think?"

Mum answered him, "I agree. I don't really like the name 'Belle'. She's not really a 'Belle'. So, what should we call her?"

Mum and the Captain thought for a long time, trying to come up with the perfect name. "We should call her 'Floppsy'. She's always flopping over so we can scratch her tummy!" said Mum.

"No-o-o," said Captain, "that's not quite right."

"How about 'Sneezy' because she's always sneezing?"

"She's not one of the seven dwarves from Snow White!"

"Ummmm ... what about 'Dingdong'? She is a little goofy."

Captain laughed at that one, "I am not going through the neighbourhood calling *Dingdong! Here Dingdong* if I have to call her home! People will wonder if I'm a little odd! Let me think for a minute."

And then he sat up, snapped his fingers, and said, "How about ... Bebe?"

"I like it!" said Mum, "That's the French word for baby, and she's our baby! We'll call her Bebe!"

The sound of the new name floated over Belle's head, and felt so much better - and right - than her old name ever had.

Bebe ... The name fit in her ears just like it was made for her.

And just like that, she was Bebe.

7 - BEDS AND BEARS, BEANBAGS AND CHAIRS

Bebe was very curious about her new home. She went from room to room, looking at and sniffing everything. She walked into the bedroom first. There was the biggest bed she'd ever seen! It was huge! Bebe jumped up on it and bounced up and down, watching the cover bounce up and down with her. She found it very soft, and messed it up thoroughly as she scrambled around.

"I like this! This will be my bed!" and she curled up on a pillow to try it out. It smelled like Mum.

"Oh you are bonkers!" laughed Mum. "For tonight, you can sleep with us so your first night will not be lonely. But soon you will have your very own bed to sleep in."

Next, she explored the living room. There was a big, comfy couch, a fat cushy chair, and a leather chair that rocked. She tested all three.

"I like the chair that rocks!" cried Bebe, "When I jump on the back I can go for a ride!" So, she jumped on the back of the leather chair and rocked and rocked. That was fun!

"Uh oh," said Captain. "That's my chair! Looks like I'll have to throw a blanket over the back to protect it from your sharp claws!"

A throw was dropped over it, and Bebe jumped up on the chair again, this time with a running start. The chair rocked wildly and Bebe hung on for dear life.

"Wheeeee!! This is fun!" cried Bebe. But, of course, all Captain heard was "Me-ow, Chrrup-chrrp, me-ow!"

"Oh you are bonkers, you silly kitty!" laughed Captain.

The beanbag that she'd slept on for so long at the shelter, sat in the corner. Mum brought it home so Bebe would have something familiar to help her adjust.

Beside it, Bebe discovered a wicker basket filled with all kinds of toys. There were little balls, and mice that squeaked, and fuzzy little animals, and things with strings. Bebe love the fuzzy green mouse and carried it all over the house in her mouth.

She flung that poor mouse high up in the air. Up, up, up it went, and when it came down ... it landed right inside Mum's cup of coffee that splashed all over the place, including on her!

"Oh! What did you do now?" cried Mum.

"A-Ah-Ah**CHOO**!" Bebe let out a big sneeze from the coffee in her nose, shook her head, and ran to hide in another room.

It was a small room, with a high counter, and a funny-looking, white bowl-thingy with water in it. Bebe stood on the rim and looked inside. She reached down to touch the water. "This is a very big drinking bowl! I can drink lots now!" and she put her head right into the bowl to take a drink!

"No, no!" cried Mum, "you can't drink out of the toilet bowl! Oh, you are bonkers!" She picked Bebe up off the toilet seat and gave her a wee pat on the behind. The lid was put down so she couldn't drink that water again.

Next, Bebe went exploring upstairs in the loft. Besides the big loft, there were two other smaller rooms up there. One had a cushy bed

which she messed up too, and the other small room had another big bowl-thingy that Mum called "toilet". Bebe had a quick drink, although it didn't taste very good.

In the loft itself was a desk with lots of pencils and papers on it. The pencils were fun to play with, and she batted them around until all of them went flying off the desk and landed on the floor. Flying pencils! What better game could there be?

The papers were next. By the time Captain came upstairs to see what that bonkers kitty was doing, there she was, standing on a perfectly cleaned up desk.

"See? I fixed the mess!" said Bebe proudly.

"Come back downstairs and play with your own toys!" cried Captain.

But I'm not finished playing here yet!" said Bebe, as she looked for more things to swat around.

But, of course all Captain understood was, "Me-ow, chrrup-chrrp, me-ow!"

There was one more room downstairs that Bebe hadn't checked yet.   The door stood open. Bebe ducked through before Mum could stop her. "Oh! You want to check out this room too? OK, go ahead."

The first thing she saw was another bed. She checked it out, to see if it bounced, and yes, it was another bouncy bed that made her very happy. It was now also very messy.

And then ... *then* ... Bebe saw them! Teddy bears! Lots and lots of teddy bears, sitting on shelves in the corner of the room. So many fuzzies in one place! Oh my! Bebe almost got dizzy.

If she jumped onto the window seat and stretched, she could reach and pull one off the shelf to play with. Which she did. Over and over. Before anybody knew what was happening, Bebe had dragged all the teddy bears out of the room to be scattered all over the hallway so she could play with them.

"How did all my teddy bears get out of the room and into the hallway?" Mum asked nobody in particular.

Was it Mum who did it?

Nope.

Was it Captain who did it?

Nope.

There was only one culprit, and everybody knew how those teddy bears ended up on the floor in the hall.

"Bebe! Those are my teddy bears!" cried Mum. "Oh my, you are bonkers! I'll have to get you your own teddy bear to play with."

All the bears were picked up and put back on the shelf in the room with all the teddy bears, and the door was firmly closed. From then on Bebe checked every day to see if the door to that room was open, and if it was … well, the bears always made a not-so-mysterious trip to the hallway, or even to the living room!

Finally, Bebe was a little tired from all the exploring. She needed a nap, big-time. She walked to the beanbag which smelled just like the

shelter, but it wasn't quite right anymore. Bebe couldn't say why. All those long months she had slept in the beanbag, and it always felt right. But now, it just didn't.

She saw Captain sitting in the leather chair that rocked. Without another thought she climbed into his warm lap and curled up.

"Yes, this feels just right!" mumbled Bebe, and fell fast asleep.

But of course, all Captain understood was, "Meow, chrrup-chrrp, me-ow."

The End ~ for now …

the adventures will continue!

BONKERS, BEHIND THE SCENES

One of the first photos of Bebe in her new home. She spends a lot of time on the windowsill …

… because it's right above the heat register!

Definitely Captain Bill's cat. He's her go-to person. When the Captain is in his chair, there she is, on his lap, always.

Loves everybody …
can you tell?

Also loves sunshine,
and stealing teddy bears!

ABOUT THE AUTHOR

Elly Mossman lives in the Cowichan Valley, on Vancouver Island, BC, and is the author/illustrator of the ongoing graphic novel-style kids' book series *Grampa Was an Alien.* Other books include, *Wait .. WHAT?* (a humorous semi auto-biography),*The Ballad of Blue Eagle Bill,* (an illustrated epic children's poem), and the full-length graphic novel, *Nmp-Chks & Numskuls.* She also does serious work such as oil paintings, graphite and conté drawings, and portraits, both human and animal.

Awards include those from the annual Canadian Community Newspaper Awards, three years consecutively; category: editorial cartoons-local humour, as well as judge for the 2020 and 2021 awards. There have been many other recognitions throughout her life.

Her work includes illustrating author, Teresa Schapansky's wonderful *Along the Way* series, describing Canada, as well as *One Little Coin*, a children's book detailing the hobby of "numismatics", or coin collecting, especially written for the Royal Canadian Numismatic Association. She also illustrates for other children's authors.

She lives with her husband Bill who, on occasion, serves as an inspiration for characters in her books (Nmp-Chks & Numskuls, The Ballad of Blue Eagle Bill).

Senior cat, Bebe, the inspiration for these books, has crossed the Rainbow Bridge to chase bugs.

For more information, please visit: www.emossman.com
or contact her directly at kribldor@gmail.com.

OTHER BOOKS BY ELLY MOSSMAN

SERIES:

Grampa Was an Alien

1 – Grampa's Curious Vacation
2 – Over the Moons!
3 – The Pet Daddy
4 – Caution! Boy Ahead
5 – Comeuppance & Karma are
   Cousins
6 – My Man Ziggy

7 – Don't Trip Over the Learning Curve
8 – The Moon Shine Affair
9 – Grand Theft Saucer
10 – My Reluctant Hero
11 – The Great Underwear Caper
12 – Who's the Alien Now?

The Klaxan Chronicles

1 – The Dragons & Snogger Granx
2 – Joh-Peah's Secret

The Cat is Bonkers

Adv. 1 – Home is Not a Cardboard Box

OTHER BOOKS – KIDS

Nmp-Chks & Numskuls
the best fishing story Grampa ever told

The Ballad of Blue Eagle Bill
a fishy tall tale set into kids' poetry

'Twas the Night Before Christmas
The classic Christmas tale- illustrated

BOOKS – ADULTS

Wait, … *WHAT?*
*Non-fiction, humourous true stories, and not-so-true cartoons to tickle
your funny bone*

The Baker From Krabbendam
Biography

www.ingramcontent.com/pod-product-compliance
Lightning Source LLC
Chambersburg PA
CBHW042308080726
47818CB00035BA/372